How to look for and get a job
Manual for success

This book is dedicated
to all the nuisances I've come across along the way.
To those who have disrespected me, demonstrating the
lack of consideration for me and my work,
that have tried to throw a monkey wrench in my works,
and that didn't believe in my good intentions.
I'm grateful and I forgive you,
because thanks to you,
I had the necessary material
to write this manual.

Acknowledgements

Thanks to Miriam, my family and friends,
for having always been present.

Ever tried? Ever failed? No matter. Try again. Fail again. Fail better.

S.Beckett

Introduction

Dear reader,

this is a very special book that will guide you "pedetemptim" as the latins said (step by step) towards the work you so desire.

I could compare it to a satellite navigator, which takes you to destination, indicating the shortest route with least traffic, although you have never been there before.

Has been written taking care of every last detail with extreme precision, to make this book effective; just as you would like your nuclear radiation suit to be produced if you unfortunately find yourself crossing a heavily contaminated area.

It's largely autobiographical, and tells about my experiences (gained in over twenty years) in the role of candidate looking for job in Italy and abroad, but also in the role of recruiter.

I've always wanted a book like this,

because it would have allowed me to save time and effort, overcoming easily the pitfalls of selections.

Certainly, by reading and putting into practice what I told in the pages of this book, you will greatly increase your chances of achieving your goals.

Often, having studied and being prepared in your own field is not enough; in a sport like football (for example), there are teams and players that play very well, but keep in mind that always wins the match who scores the goal.

This book contains suggestions, real events and things that nobody will tell you.

It offers an overview of what you need to know from the beginning of the job search, providing the analysis of all the phases of the selection process, up to the conclusion. Doesn't go into details for single topic (perhaps a book would not be enough for everyone…!), but the very interesting thing is that you know that it exists, and if you desire, you can go deeper in what interests you most.

You will avoid running into "traps" lengthened to the

candidates during the interviews and you will learn to defeat the distrust of recruiters towards you, by lowering that "virtual drawbridge" that each of us keeps raised against those we do not know.

You will be able to dedicate your best energies and your time (which unfortunately nobody gives back to you), to build solid results.

Enjoy the reading and good luck!

Contents

Chapter I
The quest: where, how and when search

To understand where to start, you need to ask yourself some questions to better define everything and avoid wasting time.

Let's start with the question: "**where** do I want to work, in which territory?" (city, province, Italy, Europe, world).

In fact, depending on the job you are looking for, a large city of international scope, will certainly offer you more possibilities than a country with few inhabitants.

Pay attention, because you will have to evaluate well the relationship between the salary offered and the cost of living in the city where you would like to move.

It's useless for you to move to another city if at the end of the month, your salay starts passing from hand to hand leaving you with nothing left in your pocket, once fixed costs are removed; you run the risk of becoming the gear of a stable mechanism (theirs), settling down (to remain forever) in the tranquility and security of a permanent job, but that won't get you anywhere.

You must also consider age; if, for example, you are between 18 and 25 years old, you can safely launch into an experience abroad that will surely help you grow both professionally and in life.

If you don't feel well, you can always go back and resume your previous route or change your goal.

If you are between 30 and 40 years old (and beyond, because you can always start over), you are probably already professionally prepared and are looking for something better for you or want help your children (if you have any) to build their future in a place that offers more possibilities; in this case the choice must be weighted more, taking into consideration all the difficulties connected with the transfer.

If you already have a city in mind where you would like to move, start documenting (today with the internet it's so easy) you should search and follow blogs and pages of people who have already moved to that city (and have lived there for years), in order to have an anticipation of difficulties they had to face. You must collect as much informations as possible, especially in case of transfer abroad, so as to cushion the impact with the change of life, **culture** and **laws**.

You will need to be ready to <u>accept and respect the culture and laws</u> of the state in which you are going to live and work.

Another factor that shouldn't be underestimated, is the climate one; in fact, it's easier to move to a city where the climate is favorable compared to that of the place where you live, rather than in other places where it rains continuously, the sun rarely shines and maybe during the winter the temperatures drop to twenty degrees Celsius below zero!

In this regard, I'm going to tell you a story that really happened.

I'll call the italian guy with a fancy name, let's say Piero, which is a name that appeals to me!

After a few years working for italian companies, he decided to move to London at the age of 27/30;

beautiful city and forge of famous rock bands. I added this detail, because being Piero a discreet musician as well as multi-instrumentalist from a very young age, he dreamed of breaking into the world of music by pursuing this passion, in parallel with a stable job.

Piero, had found a job in line with the skills he had studied for and knew the current whife from whom, shortly thereafter, he would have expected a child.

Photos and spectacular posts on social media, research and transfer to a larger house, and down to paint the walls of the room for the unborn child.

And yet in all this, a nice picture, in Piero's thoughts there was something out of place… like a small group of off-key notes, inside a perfect symphony.

You will say me, Riccardo you can't have everything!

Won't you want your cake and eat it too?!?!

Shortly after the birth of the son, maybe a year (I don't

remember exactly) Piero decided to leave London, with the whole family in tow.

I bet you also now want me to tell you what happened to Piero…!

First of all, let's take two steps back.

Piero spent his youth in an italian city overlooking the sea, where basically winter (the real one) never existed, and the weather was always sunny with scarce rains.

For this, before ending up as the frog in the pot (which finds the lukewarm water pleasant by continuing to swim, not caring about the fact that it gradually becomes warmer and not having jumped out of the pot in time, ends up cooking and dying), becoming too distracted by the beautiful general picture and by now tired of the London climate, Piero decided to abandon the splendid London, to move to a city on the sea in Australia.

Then please, don't underestimate the climate factor

because in the long run, as far as the spirit of adaptation you can have, it could seriously "affect" your happiness/serenity.

The important thing is that you understand in time the cause of what is preventing you from feeling at your best.

Moreover it is useless to tease oneself by trying to convince oneself that the situation in which we have entered cannot be improved or modified because we have reached an advanced stage of the same.

An alternative solution, as our friend Piero has taught us, is always possible.

Just as the sailor adjusts the sails when the wind changes, Piero also preferred to change course before the age advanced too much, risking ending up in the pot and avoiding finding himself old and not being able to venture into a new city, looking for a better (if not perfect) life.

Let's move on to how to **search**.

The possibilities are many; I will try to list them in order of, pass me the military similarity, "range".

It starts from the "Job posting" inside the company where you are already working, passing by word of mouth between acquaintances and friends, up to the announcements published on paper newspapers and job search websites in your area of residence or in other cities.

This, if you are actively looking for job.

As an alternative, you can register on job search sites, or on work-related social networks by specifying the desired profession and actively participate in reactions to posts and comments in groups and forums relevant to your professional sector (or even different from yours if you have decided to undertake a new career path).

There are also sites of temporary employement agencies and by registering, you can always be updated on the current selections and be contacted directly if you have skills that are sought by companies.

Based on my personal experience, many companies rely on temporary employement agencies for the following reasons:

- select the candidates to fill a vacant position (fixed-term or permanent), since they don't have a human resources office that can take care of them.
- do not hire permanent staff.
- being able to fire from one day to the next if the workload is reduced or for any other reason.
- periodically renew the staff to receive contributions (in Italy at least) for training and new hires.
- have staff available to be squeezed to the maximum every day (doesn't matter if the employee runs out physically or mentally) since will be replaced in the short term.
- cover shifts of the staff who are on vacation and / or sick.

The "recruiters" of these agencies are very clever at convincing people; they know how to sell well.

I want to warn you that the seller always knows what he is selling, while the buyer doesn't always knows what he is buying.

They could tell you that many workers started as temporary workers and were stabilized later on with the permanent contract… (although they probably already know that the company they are selecting you for, needs a worker for only 4 months and at the end of this period you will be informed that unfortunately the conditions that were created at the time of signing your contract have changed… how strange!).

Another example really happened; after seven months of work with an interim contract, I received this message on my mobile phone near the end of the last renewal granted by law:

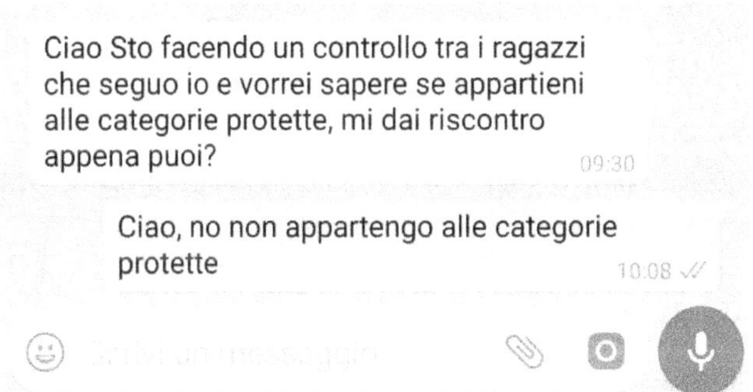

"Hi, I'm doing a check among the guys that I follow and I would like to know if you belong to sheltered groups, you give me feedback as soon as you can?"

"Hi, no I don't belong to sheltered groups".

Probably, the client company was looking for resources belonging to sheltered groups in the list of hired technicians, to have tax breaks for the transformation of the contract from interim to permanent.
Needless to say, at the end of the interim contract I had become an innocent victim of a dismissal.
In reality, the temporary employement agency knew full well that the client company would employ eclusively resources belonging to sheltered groups,

but was careful not to let me know.

I came to know this information from a very dear former colleague, belonging to sheltered groups, who was hired with transformation of the contract from interim to permanent, the year before I set foot in the company.

Having know this before, I wouldn't have wasted my time or run for the job and not even worked at it.

I wanted to tell this episode, to update you on certain "mechanisms".

You don't know everything in a situation; it is possible that someone is withholding the information from you, or that you have not been given all of the facts.

It's clear that the recruiter knows well all the informations and is in a position of advantage over you; watch out for the wolf in sheep's clothing!

So you need to weigh every information well and decide very carefully to avoid big disappointments.

The trial period is sufficient to see how you work.

After that, either the employee is hired or sent home.

Surely we must be positive, but not naive.

You are reading this book that I wrote, to turn you into successful candidates and not to being deceived by the talk of four crafty ones.

Please note that the above, has been personally tested in over twenty years of work experience in Italy and abroad.

The same experiences were also witnessed to me by former colleagues who couldn't help but confirm the above.

Meeting them on the street, they told me:"I don't understand why my contract has not been renewed… I have always worked well…!".

And then, go and and explain during a job interview that you have worked for some companies with interim contracts and nobody hired you with a permanent contract.

Because you would seem the strange one, when instead it's the system that is all wrong.

Healthy companies, enter into permanent contracts with increasing safeguards, the others either in bad faith or managed by ignorant; forget about.

In any case, now that I've opened your eyes, I suggest you always to accept a job when it's offered to you; Because whatever the duration (one week, one month, one year), the experience gained will help you grow and improve in your professional career.

Another thing that puzzles me, is the fact that the companies that use temporary employment agencies to search their employees, tend to hide themselves.

In fact (at least in Italy) you will know the name of the company only after a first cognitive interview sustained at the temporary agency and if you'll decide to go ahead with the selection.

Once decided where you want to work and understood how to identify the work, we can move on to "**when**" to look for it.

I state that every time of the year is undoubtedly valid to look for a job.

Based on my experience, I have noticed that many companies concentrate staff searches in two periods of the year; the first, between the end of the year and the first months of the new year (let's say from december, until mid-february).

The second, from the last week of august (month in which in Italy almost everything stops for vacations and many members of the staff are not in the office to participate in the selection), until mid-october.

However, there are also exceptions; for example, if an employee goes on maternity leave, sickness for medium/long periods, decides to leave the company because has found better, or retires.

In these cases, the company will begin the selection process in order to urgently replace the employee for a determined or permanent period of time, depending on the cases.

Now that we know wich are the best periods to look for a job, doesn't mean that during the rest of the year we should remain idle.

I suggest that you spend some time each morning scrolling through job postings, and monitor companies you would like to work for, to promptly check new opportunities.

Chapter II
Cover letter and CV

Have you ever seen the docking maneuvers of a ship at the port? No?

No problem, I'll tell you.

When the ship slowly approaches the quay, the sailor prepares the large ropes (hawsers) that will be needed to secure the ship to the bollards on the quay.

The hawsers, however, being very heavy, are difficult to lift (let alone to throw) and would fall into the water making it impossibile for the mooring operator the job on the quay.

To help the task, the hawser is tied to a much thinner rope called sàgola (heaving line).

The sailor throws the heaving line at the mooring operator who is waiting for him at the dock and once the latter has grabbed it, he lets drop down the hawser from the ship and it's retrieved from the water by the heaving line and then secured to the bollard by the mooring operator through a couple of turns (or simply lipped on the bollard if it has an eyelet).

Every time you send your CV, make sure it is always

accompanied by a cover letter.

Otherwise, it would be like trying to throw the hawser at the mooring operator… your CV would "fall" into the sea with no possibility of being recovered by the recruiter.

The cover letter will be your "heaving line", and will allow you to approach the recruiter through your introduction, and then going on with the story of our work experiences reported on the CV (your hawser) to ensure that your "ship" will dock to the interview without difficulties.

I talked about the importance of the cover letter, because it represents your business card and gives a preview on what a recruiter will read on your CV.

I'll not loose time about the steps to write a spectacular cover letter or an outstanding CV.

I learned by experience that the perfect CV or the universal cover letter doesn't exist.

It's necessary to personalize them from time to time like a tailored suit, highlighting the qualities and values we possess, based on what the company in wich you're aspiring to work for, is looking for.

Make sure your CV matches the job, role, industry and

sector you're applying for.

However, there are some rules that you cannot ignore when writing a cover letter and a CV.

The first one is the **order**; check that there are no spelling errors, verify text formatting and that everything reported is correct.

The second one is **readability**; choose a character that is easily readable (for example: times new roman, verdana, etc. etc.) and make sure that the size of the character is decent, so that the recruiter is not forced to use the magnifying glass, if he should print it out (best to avoid 8 character).

Do some printing proofs and verify that the characters aren't too small to read.

After submitting your CV and cover letter, take a screenshot (save an image of what is displayed on your screen) of the ad for which you're applying.

Or if you prefer, save the text of the advertisement.

It's really important, because if they should call you for an interview, you will be able to re-read (indeed you will have to) the description of that advertisement.

In fact, the description, contains the qualities required to fill the role sought in a given company and you will also find all the information to deal with the interview.

I suggest to create a main folder, which you can name for example "candidacies" or "work" and inside create sub-folders with the name of the company and the date of application.

Inside each folder, save the cover letter and the CV used to apply (wich must be customized for each company) and the screenshot of the advertisment you have responded, as mentioned earlier.

Chapter III

Interview preparation and how to face it

Section I – Discovering informations about the company, HR staff and define who you are

To find informations about the company, unless you already know it, internet is a great tool.

You can check on the company's website, type of products or services it provides, check whether it's a young and expanding company (or if already consolidated but undergoing renewal) and the future targets.

Regarding the informations about HR personnel, with whom you will be interviewing, you must investigate and act as an hacker would.

Write a list of key people in the organization, who are responsible for selecting personnel.

If nobody has told you the names and surnames of the people you're going to meet at the interview, look for them on the internet... everything is more or less easily to found.

The next step, will be collect informations about their interests on all social networks, from the most used to the less famous.

Naively, lots of people leaves social network's profiles open (with very low privacy settings) and therefore, it becomes very easy for anyone collect informations about people's hobbies and interests.

Hackers use this informations to tease the attention of the "target victims" by preparing emails with viruses attached; you instead, will use them as a hook to capture the attention of recruiters during the interview, telling episodes that fit perfectly with their pastimes.

Practical example:

Did you find out that your recruiter posted some photos of him in the stands during a soccer match?

Are you applying for a position where you will join a working group?

You'll tell that back in the days, as a boy, you had a lot of fun playing football with friends and that through this sport you learnt how important is teamwork

to score a goal and then reach the targets!
In this way, you will fascinate and generate attraction in
your interlocutor.

Re-read the curriculum several times and train yourself to
exhibit your study, work and life experiences, highlighting
your professional and personal abilities, acquired during
the journey of life.
You will have to know how to sell your talent well,
promoting you to the recruiter and highlighting that you
have the characteristics to fill the vacant position.

Section II - Clothing, cleaning, education and good manners; "landing" the interview

Since the human body is covered for 9/10 by clothing it's from the latter that you have to start.

Some say that the suit don't make the monk, but they're very often wrong, especially if in the company where you want to be hired, there is a dress code (for example a jacket and tie).

If they have already set you a date for the interview, I suggest to go to the company headquarters a couple of days before, for two reasons.

The first, is to time the time you will need to get there and evaluate the traffic in the area (whether you have a private car/motorbike, for wich you must also considerate the time for finding a parking space, whether you are using a public transport vehicle); in this way, you will avoid presenting yourself at the last minute in a state of agitation, or even worse late, all sweaty and / or out of breath.

Of course this check must be made at the same schedule as the interview was scheduled, as it would not make sense to go there for example at 9:00 pm, a time in which there may be less traffic than at 8:00 am (time when many go to work or take children to school and could happen to be slowed down by some traffic jam).

It's a good idea to arrive at least 10/15 minutes before the scheduled time, to settle in and make yourself comfortable before meeting the recruiter.

<u>The second</u>, is to spend time near the company as "investigators", to observe the kind of clothing used by employees and copy it (or take inspiration) for the day of your interview.

If you are shy, you can sit comfortably in your car and pretend to read a newspaper, otherwise (to observe the clothing closely) you can ask for informations to one of the employees at the entrance, about an office (even imaginary) recently transferred near the company.

You'll need to seem, as much as possible, like the kind of employee who "circulates in the company", in this way, you'll give the recruiter the sensation that you've always been part of that environment.

People <u>likes those like them</u>; I'll talk about it later on.

Anyways, the day of the interview, be elegant! And even if you usually use the tracksuit to go shopping because you are more comfortable, make a little effort and at least for the interview… be elegant!

As suggested by a music teacher during a lesson, in the years when I attended the conservatory of music, wear at home the dress you'll use on stage (you at the interview) and do some walk at home, so as not to be clumsy in the movements; the dress will start shaping on your body.

Same thing for the shoes, especially if they have leather sole, you'll begin to consume them a bit (thus avoiding unpleasant slips) and they will soften after the first steps; furthermore, if you fell pain in your ankles, you can take off your shoes immediately and know in time that you will need an adhesive plaster to protect your ankle (rather than feel pain during the interview).

Another suggestion, this time only for women;

don't exaggerate with accessories, rings, bracelets and necklaces (you aren't going to the disco or to a party with your friends).
The focus, must be on what you have to say.
It's really important communicate, even through elegant clothing, a feeling of reliability and sobriety.

I'll make a general overview and some examples about how people get's influenced by the colors on a psycological level (as demonstrated through the choices of many companies for their logos), to arrive at the colors recommended for the clothes; you will then go deeper through the web, books or magazines, if the topic should arouses more curiosity.
Brown is chosen very often for the furnishings of bars and pubs because they say it's the most suitable to entice potential customers to stay in the room, transmitting them a feeling of comfort.
Orange, a color chosen by a famous multinational

company for its logo, is associated with audacity.

Green is a reassuring color; if, for example you are entering a road with your car, it's most likely that motorists would be more likely to let you pass if you are driving a green vehicle rather than a gray or a black one.

Yellow is associated with madness by experts.

Red is considered the color of passion, but is often used to indicate dangerous situations; for example the red light or the red buoys at the exit of a port, from which one must keep distant.

Having introduced the topic of colors, let's see which ones are the best suited for the clothing to wear at an interview.

We are immediately helped by bees, who prefer the colors of nature.

The colors in the picture on the next page summarize the above and are among those recommended for clothing to wear at the interview; the blue of the sky, white (neutral color, for example a beautiful white shirt) and green.

Just as bees do not appreciate the black color, do not wear it for an interview, because it's considered a color that makes you nervous (and not just bees).
If don't believe me, you can always get closer to a beehive, wearing a black t-shirt or a black garment… but be aware, that I don't take any responsibility for the consequences!
Last but not least, the blue color indicates precision and creates a sense of trust and security;

it's often used in banking environment and / or insurance companies.

Here are some informations (which unfortunately aren't obvious for many).
Take care of hygiene, dress yourself clean and neat; short and clean hand nails for the boys and, well-groomed if long and glazed for the girls.
Don't bite your nails!
Avoid exaggerating with make-up on your face or even with perfume.
Well-combed and clean hair.
Use a good deodorant after the shower and, later on, give one squirt of perfume just before getting out of the car and present yourself at the interview.
Last but not least, clean teeth for a dazzling and reassuring smile.
No chewing gum!

Section III – About the form / forms to fill before the interview

The great day has finally arrived!
Before going to the interview (or if you prefer, the night before), print a copy of your CV and take it with you, for two important reasons.
The first one, is that sometimes as soon as you arrive at the interview venue, a form is delivered to fill in with your data, where you have to list your work experiences; so, as example, if you have worked for 10 seasons in 10 different hotels, will be easier to list and describe the tasks performed and the exact dates of beginning and end of each season.
You may say… "What's the point of printing a copy if I can consult it from my cell phone?".
Here we are with the second reason; during the interview it is not "hygienic" to see the candidate looking for something in his cell phone.

Even if you're in good faith, while browsing your CV electronically, the recruiter could think that you're minding your own business, chatting with your girlfriend or answering your friends about the restaurant you would prefer for saturday night dinner... could interpret your gesture as a lack of respect for his work and the company he is representing, perceiving little interest from you in getting the job.

To avoid slipping on this banana peel, print your CV and keep it in your pocket, you may need it.

Another thing that I have never liked about these modules, is that sometimes it's required to indicate the profession of the parents; and then for what?!?!

It is you, who have applied for the job, not your parents; and if you're trying to get this job, simply means that you need it.

Please be careful because it's a trap!!!

Unfortunately we live in an era of social envy, and the ignorance (or worse the hatred) of some recruiters could severely penalize you.

Reading that you are, for example son of a lawyer, the recruiter will imagine some scene from a movie where you see those prestigious law firms inside the skyscrapers of New York.

Believing that your family is very rich, will discard you in a blink of an eye, discriminating you compared to other less prepared candidates, with less desire to work, and perhaps with less need of a job… but who have been more clever and careful to traps!

Maybe your father is a lawyer and has trouble due to the decrease in business volume; probably to raise money, he had to sell the studio he had purchased with enormous sacrifices and now receives at home his customers to cut the expenses.

Same thing if you are the son of an entrepreneur; perhaps in reality he is overwhelmed by debts and doesn't know how to pay his employees at the end of the month.

Instead, the recruiter might think that you are the family offspring, go out with luxury cars, designer clothes and that two or three times a year you leave on vacation to exclusive destinations.

The recruiter doesn't have complete visibility of the scenario you are in, and this could be to your detriment.

I absolutely don't understand why a boy should be discriminated 'cause of the job his parent does.

Be clever, like the guy who wrote "employed" in the section "parent's profession".

His father was yes, employed of a company, but earned more than the lawyer and the entrepreneur put together.

The profession employed, however, didn't rang alarm bells in the mind of the recruiter who sent the candidate forward after a first screening.

Should the recruiter ask you questions about parent's profession during the interview, <u>NEVER</u> go into details and try to bring back (always in a polite way) his attention to your job experiences.

Don't be fooled by a gossipy recruiter; candidates for the job are you, not your parents.

There are very rich parents out there, who don't give even a dollar to their sons.

It's unfair that the latter be penalized because of the economic conditions (apparent o real) of their parents.

Many companies, will ask you to bring some documents to the interview.

For example, a report of the activity carried out (that is a description of the structure in which you were previously inserted, function of the department in which you worked, the "vision" and the company "mission"); or (now I exxaggerate) five hundred copies of your curriculum! ☺

Whatever it is, they are asking you it for a reason. If you aren't able to follow this guidelines, or are making up excuses (because you aren't prepared) be sure that they will consider this as an indication of how you would respond to job duties.

It could be your first assignment, don't give them a reason to throw you out before the interview.

Fly low and always give your best.

Chapter IV
During the interview step by step

As soon as you arrive, introduce yourself and greet cordially those who welcome you with a smile and shake your hand (I recommend, a firm but not excessive handshake, and not too weak… you aren't passed out!); do not hold the handshake too long (over three seconds).

Remember that in every company, to get to any office, you must first go to the usher… a word is enough to the wise!

If they make you sit down, waiting for the recruiter to be ready to receive you, wait patiently without showing annoyance (please, keep the facial expressions and be careful not to do anything that could be misunderstood and / or reported to the recruiter).

In fact, from the moment you set foot inside the building where the interview will take place, you are under examination.

Once inside the room where the "interview" takes place, in case of individual interview, say hello shaking hand with the recruiter or those present if there were more than one person; if it were a whole team of people ready to know the future colleague, it will be enough to say:"good morning to everyone (or good evening)", with a smile.

Same thing, in case of a group interview (that is, with several candidates in the room at the same time), greet each other by saying:"good morning / good evening to everyone", accompanying the greeting with a slight smile.

Let us now return to the individual interview; from this moment, the actual interview begins, so you will have to **read** and **react** at the right moment to the signals of the recruiter during the interview or you will become dead flesh in the jaws of the lion.

This means that you will have to keep the goal you need to achieve, always in the forefront of your mind.

Be serene, answer the questions correctly and also have a look to what is happening around you; look at the facial expressions of the recruiter, evaluate his interest for you, keep an eye on his arms (if are tightly folded accross his chest, and chin down, it isn't a good sign... probably the recruiter is on the defensive or feels insecure on an unconscious level!).

In the real world there will never be perfectly identical job interviews, no matter how many rehersal you will mentally do previously.

I open an important parenthesis (and ample.. I'll try to be brief as far as possible, because a whole book would not be enough on the subject).

Let's start with the basic concepts present in the life of every human being: pleasure and pain.

We seek **pleasure**, and **avoid pain**.

If an encounter with you is distasteful because it generates revulsion or brings down the people, guess what happens when that person has the opportunity to encounter you next time?

He will avoid you, crossing the street or hiding behind some supermarket shelve, because you suck.

No matter how you have been treated in your life,

the garbage that they always threw at you and the things you have to endure every day; nobody cares.

I recently saw a video on social media, in which a taxi driver is insulted by the driver in front of him, for having sounded the horn, asking him to free the road.

Instead of getting upset, the taxi driver starts laughing, causing great amazement in the passenger seated behind, who asks him:"How did you stay so calm and start laughing, while the other driver yelled everything against you?".

The taxi driver looks at him in the rear-view mirror and answers:"You see, each of us carries a load of garbage, and when this load becomes excessive it tends to come out. The important thing is not to get the garbage of others thrown at you!".

So, do yourself a favor, take an envelope and put on all your trash and then store it (at least for the duration of the interview, even if you should on any occasion) in the "basement" of your mind.

You will have to attract the recruiter, that is to say, call you back for the follow up after the interview (if more steps are foreseen) or to offer you the job you're applying for.

How to generate attractiveness then, becoming real magnets?

<u>You will have to make someone feel better about themselves, as a direct result of meeting you.</u>

You could, for example, compliment yourself on how the selection procedure was handled, quickly and professionally (if it was) or explain to the recruiter that you appreciate the way to work in the company where you are applying. The important thing is that they are sincere and above all appropriate to the scenario.

I remember a few years ago, while waiting for my turn at the airport check-in, that the person before me was engaged in a discussion, perhaps due to a not allowed change of flight, towards the hostess who was there taking the screams for reasons not caused by her job, trying (uselessly) to clarify the situation to the customer.

When my turn came, annoyed by the attitude the person before me had towards the young lady, I told her not to take it personally and not to give weight to the bad words she had received, as they simply showed the low level of the "lord" in suits and ties towards those who were trying to work professionally.

Do you know what happened?

I discovered it once I got on the plane; in fact, to thank me, assigned the seat next to the emergency exit, which having no seats in front, has more space for the legs.

Another example instead, is written in this mail that I pubblish in the next page (with sender, recipient and company obscured for confidentiality):

From:	
Sent:	
To:	
Cc:	Ruggiu, Riccardo
Subject:	Riccardo in Rome

Hi 

I want to thank you very much for having let Riccardo come to Rome at my name and also for all the colleges and management!

First of all it was nice to meet him as none of us met before but I say thanks especially because he took care of lots of things and all of us had the impression that he went here also earlier as he would have been in ████ since long time ago....

Regarding me, I have to say that I had a terrible laptop with thousand issues that every morning spent 40 minutes to start and work and all day long I experienced several stops and problems with outlook especially -- calendar, contacts and mail...!

These problems were caused by no space in C disk and also by wrong or -- at least -- not proper configuration when I got this pc as new... Riccardo spent at least 4 hours with my laptop and now the baby is new and it is working much better than the day when I got it for the first time! And also he found a better RAM to install inside the laptop to get it smile ☺ faster... and I smile as well since yesterday!!!!

This is only an example to say that when Riccardo takes a problem in his hands, he doesn't leave it until it is solved in the best way... not only solved!!!

He is very professional, fast and he knows so many things.... Very deep expertise!

He also learnt to me how to feed the baby...I mean how I have to manage it in order to maintain it in efficiency!

Thanks a lot once again for all!

Regards,

I remember that I printed this email, and while I was on the train going to Pisa to spend the weekend with my girlfriend, I read and reread the content several times.

Other people practically give you back what they see, but remember that you must also be competent and professional.

I've always wanted to give people something more, through the machines I worked on; customizing and improving, for example, computers or peripherals when possible.

I believe these examples are more than enough to explain to you how to become attractive by associating pleasure with the person you meet; make a commitment to act in a way that makes people feel better about themselves after meeting you.

In the first example, I "originated pleasure" by defending the check-in attendant by enhancing her work and making her feel important after she was verbally attacked by a rude gentleman.

The same in the second example, problems that before

my "visit" in Rome were minimized (or even worse ignored, generating the experience of abandonment) by those who previously managed everything, causing frustration (and therefore pain) to the employees of an office, they were listened to and solved by generating pleasure and associating positive feelings with meeting with my person.

To recap: <u>escape from pain</u> and <u>run to pleasure</u>.
Train yourself and engage in everyday life to leave people in a better way than when you met them, by this way it will become a spontaneous habit.
Moreover, there is a famous saying which reads: "Laugh, and the world will laugh with you; cry, and you will cry alone".

Let's go back to our interview after this parenthesis.
Always keep eye contact with the recruiter; look him in the eye while exposing yours course of study and / or

work.

Don't get distracted by looking at the pictures, office furniture or objects on the desk!

Get inspired by actors in the movies, watch how they look in the eyes the person they are speaking with, when they play the role; you will have to do the same.

If you are shy, and you come uphill, look the person in eyes, fix the base of the nose… the effect will be the same.

Another fundmental thing is to show empathy; to understand what I mean, turn on the TV and watch any newscast.

Observe what the reporter does on the spot with his interlocutor while listening to the answers; in addition to holding the microphone (which doesn't interest us) and looking in his eyes, he begins to nod; usually swinging the head up and down.

In this way, he proves to be attentive to what the interlocutor is communicating to him and also puts himself in the shoes of his interlocutor proving to understand perfectly what he is telling him.

In case of positive events, a slight smile accompanies the movement of the head, while in case of negative events, he remains serious and with a frowning face.

Don't neglect the details, facial expressions are also very important.

Try to understand what you can "trace" in the other person, to enter the world of the other person.

For example you can take the last two or three words with which the other person has finished the sentence, and use them to ansie your interlocutor or to introduce a new concept (<u>verbal tracing</u>).

If, on the other hand, you have been involved in unpleasant episodes that have caused you impatience

(if you were to ask if unpleasant events were occurring in the workplace that were not caused by you, and in which you are in any case right), describe the episode that happened and, end the story with these words: "I think that anyone who found himself in that situation in my place, would have bothered".
In this way, you do the reverse procedure, that is, bring your interlocutor to "trace" your world and put him in your shoes, observing the story from your point of view.
Vice versa, when you are listening to your interlocutor you can tell him that if you were in his shoes, you would think the same way.

Pay attention to paraverbal communication and try to control yourself, because even when you are not talking, your body communicates with posture, gestures, facial expressions or even blushing due to emotional reactions (embarrasment and / or anger).

If your recruiter / interlocutor is nodding his head but in reality he is in disagreement with what you are saying, he will touch a part of the body with many nerve bundles (for example the nose). The episode just described, is an example of **cognitive dissonance**; that is, when your interlocutor pretends to be in agreement with what you are saying (nodding to not embarrass yourself), but in reality he is thinking the opposite.

An example is provided by the actor Di Caprio in the movie "The wolf of wall street"; in the first part of the film, while listening to Donnie Azoff (who tells him that he had a children with his cousin) while not agreeing with what Donnie tells him, he nods so as not to embarrass him and at a certain point he touches his nose with his hand.

Di Caprio, who is a very attentive actor to details, while he shooted this scene, voluntarily decided to make this gesture to comunicate to our unconsciuous that he actually disagreed with what Donnie was telling him, although he was nodding.

In this case, it will be our unconscious that alarms us and makes us understand that the other person does not agree with what we have just said.

Another example is the cough to "scrape" the throat.

The examples I have described are clear non-verbal signals of rejection; if one or more of these are present, you must realize that the emotional part of your interlocutor is perceiving you very negatively.

Do you know the saying "Birds of a feather flock together?"

Previously I advised you to observe the clothing of company employees, because you will have to reflect as much as possible the type of person the company is looking for.

Resume the email I published earlier, where says: "All of us had the impression that he went here also earlier, as he would have been in ….. since long time ago… "

At unconscious level you can, pass me the term, manipulate (naturally in a benevolent manner) the recruiter giving him the feeling of having known you years before.

You will have to reflect his movements / posture, his speech (slow, or fast, or with pauses here and there).

Please note that I wrote mirroring, not mimicking; in practice as if you were his mirror (repeating his gesture a few moments later).

I will now mention the <u>dynamics</u> and <u>rhythm</u> of the voice.

By dynamics, I mean the volume of your voice. Try to increase and decrease the volume of your voice as you speak, so as to transmit enthusiasm during the conversation; think of the commentary of cycling race during a 120-kilometer stage with the volume of reporter's voice always the same (and maybe the tone)… It becomes soporific!

In contrast to that of a football match, who keeps the spectator alive, with the reporter who increases the volume of the voice when the player enters the penalty area, until he shouts: "GOOOOL!".

Try to change also the rhythm of the voice, increase and decrease the speed of your speech (sometimes you also take breaks); try to convey emotions, making you attractive.

Pauses are also important; think about the comedians, who pause in silence before saying the joke of theatrical or television sketch. In that pause of a second, they hold back the curiosity of the public who breaks out laughing once they hear the joke; a bit like that "relief" that one feels when the prickling in the nose ceases after sneezing.

You will, of course, take breaks not to pronounce comic jokes, but to make them under stand (even if you already know the correct answer) that you know how to reason before speaking.

Just as the first minutes of the interview will be very important for the recruiter, who will have the maximum peak of attention in listening to you, they will also be fundmental for you in order to analyze their movements, speech and even respiratory rate if necessary.

When I learned of this technique, I didn't believe it actually worked… instead, it is often used even by the most skilled sellers and also by those who find themselves having to negotiate to achieve their goals for work situations.

According to neurolinguistic (or NLP) programming, there are three types of individuals: visual, auditory and kinesthetic. **Visual** individuals, focus on the visual observation of the surrounding world (example: "I don't see this thing well").

The **auditory** individuals, associate the sound part with the perception of the external world (exmple: "The idea of this journey, sounds interesting).

And then, there are the **kinesthetics**, that are the individuals who tend to gesticulate while they talk or need to touch the interlocutor while they talk (perhaps because of in security, or maybe to make sure they are listening to them) aaah, the tappers!

I have listed this subdivision to facilitate the recognition of the type of your interlocutor (and also to indentify yours) in order to be able to interface you in the best way and to facilitate in your favour the conduct of the interview.

Zone distances - Proxemics

To introduce the topic, I'll tell you immediately about an episode that probably happened to you too.

Here is the scenario; you are in line at the supermarket checkout and as soon as it's the turn of the person in front of you, instead of continuing by pushing the shopping cart (keeping it in front of him), he overtakes his shopping cart and "keeps you at a distance" interposing the shopping cart between him and you, as if you had a rare disease!

He simply does not want you to remain in his intimate zone (that is, from 0 to 45 cm from him), while moving the items from the shopping cart to conveyor belt of the cash desk.

Edward T-Hall, an American anthropologist, spotted 4 zone distances.

Immediately after the intimate zone, to which I mentioned in the example, we find personal zones (from 45 to 120 cm) that characterize the relationships between friends or acquaintances, that is between people with whom there is a certain confidence.

Next, we find the social zone (from 120 to 300 cm), to be adopted on formal occasions, at the job interview or business meeting.

And finally, the public area (over 3 meters) for example when meetings are held; this will involve an increase in the dynamics of the voice (to be heard better at a distance) and an emphasis on movements (to be seen from afar).

Assessment Center: what is it and how to deal with it

It's a set of tests (usually used in group contexts) in which some business scenarios are simulated, to observe the behavioral aspects of the candidates and measure their abilities and the potential suitability to fill the role relative to the ongoing selection (as example, aptitude for change, negotiation, stress management, ability in public speaking, management of a work group, etc. etc.).
Assessment centers are used by large companies, with a structured selection process.
They can last from a minimum of a one full day (starting in the morning and ending in the late afternoon), to a maximum of two / three days, to then enter the individual interview. On the web, there are examples related to the tests that are proposed during the interview; naturally exercising, you have more chances to overcome them.

Some "crafty" companies instead of the classic tests, will ask you to produce a presentation/graph with data and business statistics to assess your professional capacity… actually they want you to do a presentation (so they can get it for free) and probably have not the slightest intention to hire you (really outrageous!) but unfortunately it really happened.

You know, the consultants cost!

With regards to passing the simulation tests, you will have to rely on the "job description" (check page 17/18) and reread the skills the company is looking for, listed in the announcement for which you are candidate.

If, for example, the selection is for a "team leader", you will need to highlight your leadership and negotiation skills with your subordinates to achieve the goal.

Be very careful during the simulated tests, because you

will be observed and evaluated by professionals in the field and psychologists who will immediately notice if you are trying to cheat... even by just moving an eyebrow!

Be yourself and try to always maintain a positive attitude; if you are excited during the simulation… take advantage of these adrenaline rushes while enjoying the moment, and comunicate to your interlocutors that you feel excited about the challenge you are facing.

Chapter V
FAQ – Answers to the most frequent and worst questions

The questions listed below are (unfortunately) still frequent during job interviews.

It looks like the script of the perfect recruiter listless and little accustomed to the art of discovering the best talents (the job he has chosen and for which he receives his salary).

In my opinion, if they were to do it for you, it may be that the recruiter is new to the trade or is bored by your exposure and has listened to little and nothing of your work experiences... otherwise, guess what...? That's right, it's a piece of shit!

Dear reader, if you who are reading, are a recruiter and use the questions below during job interviews, please note that the candidate (even if he cannot say so openly) is thinking: "This is really an asshole!".

Not only that, he is also wishing you the best of the worst for your future! (I would never want to be in your shoes).

Remember that with your decision you can help those who really want to work, and the skills can always be improved; tries to perceive the candidate's potential and enthusiasm.

Do not take advantage of the scenario of psychological subjection in which the candidate finds himself, because today you have a role of power, as well as a bird that eats ants while alive; but when the bird dies, the ants eat it!

Don't underestimate anyone in life, because everything can change in a few moments and time is more powerful than you.

Returning to our discussion, the recruiter will complete the interview in an almost "mechanical" way, using these questions to end the interview in a simple way (a bit like the game of Tic-Tac-Toe).

1. *Do you have any other offers in pipeline ?*

The purpose of this question is to know whether you have submitted applications in response to other job offers.
The right answer is always and only one: No.
Remember that "No" will be fundamental in this case, even if you have submitted 50 other applications to as many companies; you will have to show the recruiter that you are focused on the job offer you are applying for. If you answer yes, you may be immediately rejected from the current selection.
Remember to always keep all doors open; if you are desperate for a job, what's the point of sending only a CV hoping for a miracle and ignoring other 50 job offers?
I believe that a professional recruiter would never ask

this question, unless he wants to check candidate's stupidity…!
It would be like asking what color was the white horse of any historical character… it makes no sense!

2. *Where do you see yourself in 5 years?*

This question is not directed to your private life, but is placed by the recruiter to try to understand your motivation and the good will to want to achieve a role with greater responsibility, in the medium/long term than that for wich you are candidates, besides contributing to the company growth.
Try to show enthusiasm and a willingness to roll up your sleeves, but be realistic.

3. *What has been your greatest failure?*

This question aims at knowing the level of awareness (of having failed) and candidate's capacity to handle responsibility.

Mention a failure and, even if it's not easy, admit it.

You may have arrived "long" by exceeding the deadline agreed with a customer for the project's delivery, or may have arrived second in the tender for the award of a contract due to an incorrect evaluation; if you are a craftsman you may have packaged the product with materials that are too cheap, and later on, have had the row of customers that after a short time, brought back the product you sold.

I could go on with many examples, but I think these are more than enough.

Explain to the recruiter what that failure taught you, the actions you have taken to get out of it and what improvements it has produced in the medium/long term following your career path.

It is normal to fail when doing something, especially when you are a beginner; is part of the experience.

As a famous Latin phrase (I still remember something, back in the classical high school days) says:"Errare humanum est, perseverare autem diabolicum". Making mistakes is human, but persevering is diabolical.

4. *We have loads of talent, why should we hire you?*

To answer this question, I refer you to what was mentioned in the second chapter and in the third crapter section 1.
Reread the screenshot of the job offer; in fact in the description, the qualities that the company seeks are reported.
Check the company's website again, to memorize comany's goals, its values and the type of products and/or services it manages.
Once you have this information clear, you will have to promote and sell yourself, explaining to your interlocutor that not only you can bring to the company the skills and expertise he is looking for, but you are also able to do the tasks better than others.
Put yourself in the shoes of the selector and think about what he would like to hear; you must highlight the way in which <u>you can be useful to the company first</u>.
So prepare a beautiful presentation about yourself, telling it effectively (by underlining your strengths, in common

with what the company is looking for) the experiences listed in the resume and also the extra-work experiences that bring out other skills / competences developed.
To complete what was said above, you can tell an episode (not necessarily occurring in the workplace) in which you have successfully achieved your goal.
Remember to keep yourself always positive and to generate enthusiasm in those who are listening to you.

- short parenthesis about humilty -

I noticed that people do not understand the concept of humility.
For example, you will hear: "That footballer is humble".
You will answer: "It doesn't seem very humble, since he drives a 210.000$ SUV and not a 10.000$ car".
They will tell you again: "Yes, because he can afford it".

All this puzzles me… and I think that the footballer, after all… isn't so much humble!
Maybe he is a bit crafty, he greets all his fellow citizens even if he doesn't know them (preaching well) but then he drives around the city in a car that is anything but modest (scratching badly).

The job world (that nowadays is unfortunately scarce in Italy, but also in the rest of the world), is comparable to an ocean full of scharks.
Imagine yourself diving into a place that (unbeknownst to you) is well populated with sharks; do you think they will spare you because you are humble people?
They will tear you to pieces in no time!
Do yourself a favor and when you find yourself among the sharks, leave the humility at home; exaggerated!
With this, I'm not saying that you have to be conceited and arrogant.
You have to show decision and security, guaranteeing maximum availability if you are required to attend training courses for learning company procedures, rather than to

fill a missing competence in your resume or possibly improve it.

5. What would your old boss say about you?

This question aims to know what an old boss thinks about you, and winks at your self-esteem.

In my case, I would answer by quoting part of the feedback email published on page 40: "This is just an example to say that when Riccardo takes a problem in his hands, he does not leave it until it is solved in the best way… not only solved!!!

He is very professional, fast and knows so many things… a very deep experience!".

If you are a precise and punctual person, you can communicate these qualities.

Always keep in mind the philosophy and objectives of the company to which you are proposing, before telling what strengths it would list of you, your former boss.

6. What is your biggest weakness?

Is there anybody who has no weaknesses?

I really don't think so…!

Talk about some flaws or bad habits that have no impact on the job for which you are proposing yourself.

If, for example, the job position requie that you hold speeches in front of large crowds in open spaces, tell the recruiter that you are perfectly at ease when you speak to a public of two hundred people but you feel uncomfortable when you have to talk to five people during a meeting in an office.

In this way, you will provide an adequate answer without evading the question.

7. Do you have any questions for us?

The right answer is always YES!
Prepare a series of questions pertinent to the company and type of work, but be careful not to ask questions about the salary, in particular if it's the first meeting-interview.

If instead the subject of the salary is introduced by the recruiter and asks you to propose your rate, just comunicate one in line with your experience and point out that in any case, you are willing to find an agreement.

Landscape's view it's important

Every now and then, even if I'm working, I like to propose myself to companies to keep me in training and, at the same time verify what skills are required by the job market.

It happened to me a long time ago to hold an interview, and find myself in an unpleasant situation because of the scarce propensity of recruiters (who dedicated themselves to interviewing me) to be up to date.

Dealing with new technologies, I was asked which of three competitors I would choose to do an email migration on cloud-based servers.

After having thought for a few moments, I proposed what I thought could be best, initially arousing an amused murmur of disagreement by these three "pseudo-recruiters", who then replied to my answer by claiming that the competitor I indicated did not provide cloud mail management service.

This interview took place in march and the competitor I

indicated, begun offering the cloud mail management service during october of the previous year.

Unfortunately the recruiters were not up to date and in their heads, the correct answer was another, because of their obsolete beliefs.

It's clear that I had a view of the landscape different from that of my interlocutors and even if I had said that the service of this company was available from october of the previous year, I would not have been believed because they had fossilized on old information, not updating themselves.

<u>People only believe what they know</u>, and it's very difficult to change their beliefs.

In situations like this, keep calm even if you probably have the worst thoughts in your mind.

Answering back or worse still insulting the recruiters, you would pass in the wrong.

Besides, remember this phrase: "<u>Always allow others to save face</u>".

These three gentlemen turned out to be three "heads of nothing" and without having shown a shred of respect for the candidate (who at that time was me, but could have been anyone).
After the interview, I was honestly annoyed by that episode; but later I was happy, thinking that working with such characters would have been a real hell.
They were revealed for what they were; unprofessional people (because not updated, in a sector where technologies change from one day to the next).
Coming out of that interview, it was a great liberation for me and I still consider myself very lucky.
I had learned a very important lesson; landscape's view is not the same for everyone.
When describing a situation, an object, a scene, try to bring the greatest possible details of the photograph (or if you prefer of the painting) that you have in mind.

Because your interlocutors, come from paths of life,
studies and work eperiences different from yours and
therefore what for you can be simple and obvious, for
others it is not.
Try to describe everything as completely as possible
without leaving out any details (in the case of my
experience, the october date of the previous year) as if
the interlocutor started from scratch and was ignorant on
the subject.

Chapter VI – Timing and various questions
Timing & Latence

At the beginning of each day, as well as every action, everything takes place according to the timing. For example at the theater or in the cinema, there are timing of acting (the pauses that the comedians make before the joke that triggers the laughter of the audience) or the timing of drying a car's paint inside the oven of a car body shop.

And then there is latency, an interesting word that means this: "Time that elapses from the moment an action is requested and its actual execution".

It can be high, or low. For example, a man who drives drunk, will have a high latency (slow reflexes) in braking a vehicle and will be much more dangerous than a sober driver who will be able to promptly stop the vehicle (low latency) in an emergency situation by avoiding an impact on a wall or another vehicle posing a serious danger to his own life and that of other drives.

Unfortunately (or fortunately, depending on the case) these two factors are also part of the job search/selection phase.
How long does the recruiter have to call me since I sent him the resume?
And above all, will someone call me?
But is the resume read? Or is it trashed directly?
How long does an interview last?
Will they give me feedback after the interview?
How long do I have to wait to consider the selection concluded, or to know if there will be a sequel?
I respond with immense pleasure to these questions, because it's not pleasant to remain in a limbo to wait without knowing what is happening, perhaps waiting for a response that will never come; is not beautiful.
I'll tell you on the next pages, based on my direct experience.

*- How long does the recruiter have to call me,
since I sent him the application?*

My personal record from the moment I sent the application to a job offer (in another city where I don't reside and I am not even domiciled) to when I was called from a recruiter by phone, is 7 minutes!

Honestly, when I answered the phone, I thought it was someone who wanted to sell me something.

This is a rare episode, so much so that the selector himself told me: "I know it will seem strange to you, but I'm calling you for the position you applied a few minutes ago!".

Other times, happened to send the application at 10:00 a.m. in the morning, and be called back in the afternoon of the same day between 1:00 p.m. and 3:00 p.m.

Or it happens to be contacted the day after sending the resume (if you send it on friday and the company is

closed on saturday, they will call you on monday).
Last example is thursday and friday; final days of the week in which in the previous days a resume screening was made and the candidates are called to fix a cognitive interview for the following week.
If we consider a selection process that require two to three weeks, a correct timing is that of six/seven calendar days from sending an application.

For this and the following questions, I will establish a general rule; the <u>fifteen-day</u> rule.
In fact, this time frame is more than enough to complete the most disparate and complex assessments and, if the company that is selecting you has bureaucratic obstacles, not always linked to faults on the part of those who take care of the selection (or for example, the person with whom you are going to work closely, at the time of selection is on vacation) establishes a time frame of reference.

If your phone does not ring and you do not receive not even an email after fifteen days have elapsed from sending your application… pass on something else, they are not interested in you.

Important note, if they have to call you after fifteen days… the thing must make you trigger an alarm bell.

In fact, it may be that the initial choice made by human resources was not the right one or maybe the chosen candidate fled like hell because he did not feel well in the new work environment or accepted another job he was waiting for, taking advantage of the probation period.

Most likely, you have been called back from the list of remaining candidates.

To all this, I add an exception (from an experience I had); if they were important multinationals with very structured selection procedures and received a large number of candidates, they could call you even after twenty-seven days from sending the application.

Keep in mind thoug, that this last scenario I just

mentioned, is more unique than rare.

Now you know what happened and you can manage the choice.

My humble advice is to always try, give yourself a chance to try. If you don't try it will be a lost opportunity, always.

- *Will someone call me?*

You are not always contacted by phone, to fix the date of the interview.
It can also happen to receive an email with the indication of the date, the time and the place in which to introduce you to the interview.
If you do not receive phone calls or emails within the fateful fifteen days… move on!

- ***Is the resume read, or is it directly thrown away?***

It depends. Many companies use A.I. (Artificial intelligence) that despite the name, is (alas) actually not very smart.

If for example in the resume one or more keywords of those that have been inserted by the human resources for the research of the candidate are missing, the software will discard that curriculum.

We are talking about ATS (applicant tracking system), a software designed to help companies during the selection process.

It's used to publish a job announcement on the company website, on job search engines and on multiple social networks simultaneously; another important function is that of pre-screening which is carried out by the software, verifying the amount of keywords in the resume (as mentioned earlier) and the lack of document formatting.

Same thing unfortunately happens on a famous social network dedicated to work, and search engines of sites dedicated to finding a job.

So be careful to include in the resume the same keywords as in the description of the ad you want to answer with your application, or related to the kind of employment for which you would be called back after uploading your resume on a website of job search.

Unfortunately in this case the technology does not help, but rather, it cuts the legs even to the best professional profiles!

Imagine the scenario, a highly competent and professional person (who does not compile the resume in a way that appeals to the software who is "thrown in the meal") is immediately discarded, and instead who guesses the keywords and perhaps is not so prepared… succeeds to land the interview!

To close the speech on artificial intelligence, let me insert this quote:

"Technology is stupid unless the user is intelligent."
(Principle of the minor cunningness of Tulloch).

More than ten years ago, I asked a recruiter for advice to find out whether studying for a certificate to be added to the resume could give me a few more possibilities.
He was immediately outspoken; he replied that if he saw a certification, but there wasn't even a work experience in which the skills related to that certification had been put into practice… the resume ended up straight in the trash!

And in my opinion he wasn't wrong…! I'll make an extreme (and highly unlikely) example, but it makes a lot of it: "Would you get in the car with a driver who has a license but never held a steering wheel in his hands?".
I honestly don't.
As someone said, practice makes perfect. I believe these examples are the most pertinent, regarding the failure to read and/or consider a resume.

- How long does an interview lasts?

The duration of an interview, depends on several factors. In case you have already worked for a temporary agency and they are calling you back for a new opportunity, it will last a few minutes, just to tell you that if your CV will appeal to the company they are about to forward it to (after obtaining your consent and availability), they will call you back soon.
If they do not know you, the duration will vary from a minimum of at least twenty minutes to a maximum of over an hour, depending on how it was structured (ex. modules to be filled out, written test, cognitive chat, etc. etc.) and how many recruiters are involved.

Nowadays, it seems "old-fashioned" give the candidate feedback.

Very few companies and recruiters give feedback, so don't be surprised if they'll ignore you.

Some major multinationals, "cover themselves" and apologize in advance with a message that is displayed along with the confirmation receipt of your application.

It usually reads more or less like this: "Due to the large volume of applications received, unfortunately it will not be possible to answer everyone"; by this way, they probably feel justified.

For fairness and education, I have always provided feedback, both positive or negative when I was involved in the selection process.

Because first of all, we are people and not objects
/ gadgets to turn on and off.
Not communicating a reply is a lack of respect for those
who are looking to find a job and spent their time to write
a resume, a cover letter, and to attend the interview.
Many recruiters, prefer to disappear like ghosts (maybe
they don't know how to face situations in everyday life…
let alone at work!).
If you want, you can try with a "follow up", sending a
thank you email the day after the interview and asking for
a reply in a corteous manner.
In this way, you may receive a positive or negative
response to the outcome and / or impressions received
during the interview.

However, if the recruiter belongs to the category of "fugitive", he will escape even more!

A few years ago, I sent an email of this type to a recruiter who seemed to me correct, professional and kind.

The email was sent on thursday, and the recruiter replied that she would have had a response just the day after (Friday) by the client company with whom she had already agreed on a telephone call and would have let me know.

Neither friday nor ever, I received her feedback…!

On the same Friday, I had understood immediately the behavior of the "special" person I had met; she was a fugitive, and vanished into thin air.

It is impossible not to comunicate (Watzlawick – School of Palo Alto); even if you don't want to communicate, you are actually communicating that you don't want to communicate.

Which is still a form of communication.

Same thing, a "non-action", always corresponds to an action; you can decide not to send an email or call to give feedback and this is always an action.

To maintain calm and serenity, leave these "special" people alone, because everything in life comes back.

Set a deadline of fifteen days starting from the day of the interview.

Then, proceed like trains… always!

It will be an important step, because it will make you grow and you'll go ahead with your head held high.

While the "special" recruiter you met on your way, will fuel his childisch fugitive behavior, proving nothing but his mediocrity.

- ***How long do I have to wait, to consider the selection concluded, or to know if there will be a follow-up?***

During the interview itself, they could ask you specific questions that bode well for a sequel, such as: "Are you currently working?", "When could you start?", "What salary do you expect?".

Usually, they call you the day after the interview to tell you that it was positive and they would have the pleasure of seeing you again to start as soon as possible or to continue with the next phase of the selection process (if divided in several steps).

However, it may be that you are also the first candidate to examine (of a long list) and therefore it could take three / four days, or even a week to finish everyone's questioning.

Continuing the answer to this question, I propose again the fifteen day rule established earlier; once the deadline has been reached, and you didn't get any feedback, proceed forward with your job search. In some cases (fortunately not frequent), instead, the selection follows a more structured path through which the candidate is examined and evaluated by several people and business sectors; this can extend the duration up to a maximum of five / six weeks with the succession of more meetings.

Don't worry thoug, as the examiner on duty will inform you about this long selection process, during the first interview you'll do.

If instead they should tell you the classic phrases "Kiss of death": "We'll let you know"; or "We will make ourselves heard", remaining vague and without indicating <u>when</u> they will call you back, at 98% are not interested in you.

Why do they reject you?

I start this section with an important premise; as there are many unemployed people in each corner of the planet, it's highly probable that they will find themselves in competition with highly qualified and specialized candidates.

Unfortunately today, I see many qualified candidates who are neglected or rejected because they don't work in the same role they are applying for.

Sometimes recruiters, draw up a checklist and call the candidates who have collected the most ticks on the boxes on the list, since they seem to be the best match.

Being so tightly focused and inflexible, many companies lose employees who are great team players and innovators, who could implement new ideas to generate change and progress.

All this generates a total waste of talents that are around.

You have got the same standard rejection email: "After a careful verification of the really impressive skills and work experiences listed in your CV, we regret to inform you that this time we have preferred to direct the choice to other candidates".

Or: "Thanking you for your availability and for the time you have dedicated to us, I inform you that the skills and experiences we are looking for, are different from those, even if interesting, that you gained. Therefore, due to the current need to cover our workforce, we are not interested in starting a collaboration."

And yet, you were prepared with care for the interview and without leave nothing to chance. You had followed every suggestion step by step and you were impeccable…

And again: "we point out that the selection as ...., has been withdrawn / suspended by the client company. We will keep you in mind for future searches in line with your profile".

In the latter case, which I reported, the company thinks back about it for any reason and turns around, postponing or withdrawing the selection...!
When the company "reverses", it's absolutely not your fault and not even the recruiters; I wanted to include this possibility too, because unfortunately it happens.

First of all, don't worry and don't lose your temper; learn to accept the choice of others, who are certainly far from your way of being, from your studies and from your experiences and abilities (or unlike the text of a famous song, they aren't on your "frequency"); I urge you to explore this last concepts, according to which, every living being emits a frequency through its vibrations.

You have given your best, but unfortunately it's not always possible on all occasions to arrive first.

We can also learn this from sporting events, and we must know how to lose.

In case of a missed hiring, or failure to call for an interview, the causes can be multiple.

Having seen what happens "behind the scenes", I was able to see for myself that sometimes the differences between the competences of the candidates, are really minimal and recruiters tend to give more appreciation to some qualities of the person or to other factors, with respect to the skills which can undoubtedly be improved or integrated in case of gaps emerged from the tests.

Once, I happened to be the only one out of fifty candidates to have answered all the technical questions of the written test, correctly (100%, the maximum score) and have been included in the second group of candidates to be called back for hiring.

I came to know this information only a few weeks later, when I had already found another job.

The company had decided to hire first the candidates who had accumulated a greater period of unemployment (if I remember correctly, to get more benefits) and then all the others; all this without giving any communication to the candidates, leaving them in a limbo.

Never take it as a personal fury towards you, because you don't have the visual of the whole scenario and probably you will never know the reason for the choose of recruiters.

I'm now going to describe a sore subject and not to be underestimated… the "well-connected" people!

One often wonders why certain idiots are successful.

Bad reporters, unlikely singers, poor managers and so on (the list is long).

Most incapable people who make a career come from groups of people who exchange favors.

It's all simple, really very simple.

The more the subject is incapable, the better it's for those who command it from the upper floors, because they are more controllable and less unpredictable.

If you understand how simple the mechanism is, you will no longer be surprised to see certain situations in which imbeciles (real or apparent) cover important positions.

It will happen (hope never) to partecipate in selections, in presence of this category of people (without your knowledge); unfortunately, with good or bad manners and without you knowing it, they will overtake you, without asking anyone's permission.

A very dear friend who won a public selection and, I can guarantee you, certainly not for recommendations because he was really prepared (two graduations) and very smart, told me the following, after a couple of years spent in the new work environment: "Riccardo, there are people who are already prestigious managers before being born!".

Indeed there are people who come from important and rich families, finding themselves already with the "dish ready".

Again, you can't do anything; learn to "cash in the blow" and move on.

Try to keep your focus on yourself and do something every day (even a small thing) to always improve yourself.

Try to overcome yourself compared to the day before.

Only in this way, you'll reach new goals.

Be prepared to embrace a no, and proceed along the way without losing your precious energy, mulling over the events that have happened and cannot change; what is destined to you, will not overtake you.

If it doesn't open, it's not your door.

And concluding, like the donkey in the water well!

Like any good book, this one also has almost come to an end; but before leaving you, I will briefly summarize the history of the donkey in the well.
One day, a farmer's donkey fell into the well.
Although the farmer was fond of the donkey, the well was too narrow and deep to be able to recover it.
Since the well was now dry and the donkey was old and without strenght, he decided to bury it alive inside the well.
He summoned his neighbors to help him fill the well, throwing earth with shovels.
The donkey immediatley understood what was happening but instead of getting discouraged, for every shovels of earth that struck him, he shaked is back, causing the earth to fall and then climbing upward with the hooves.
Not long after, the now exhausted mule managed to get to the mouth of the well, cross the edge and get out.

This story teaches us a very important lesson about adversity management.

Whenever you'll not pass a selection or someone will say you no, keep this story in mind and shale off any negative considerations or scenarios; never give up!

Treasure each experience and all the criticisms you will receive, beacuse as in the case of the donkey, they will help you to get closer to your goal and in your path of human and professional growth.

RICCARDO RUGGIU was born in Cagliari in 1976.
He works in the silicon-based technology sector from over twenty years, and developed a deep experience working for the largest and major IT companies in Italy and abroad.

After publishing his first humoristic book: "Stupidario tecnico: 101 frasi dette dai clienti all'Help Desk", has devoted himself to writing this manual for the research and conquest of a job.
By the same author is also available a great book about Hi-fi: "How to buy high-fidelity".

Riccardo would love to hear about your experiences with this book (the good, the bad, and the ugly).
You can write to him at:
howtolookforandgetajob@gmail.com.